BLOOD *of* Angels

BLOOD of Angels

ALLAN SAFARIK

thistledown press

©Allan Safarik, 2004
All rights reserved

No part of this publication may be reproduced or transmitted in any form or by any means, graphic, electronic or mechanical, including photocopying, recording, or any information storage and retrieval system, without permission in writing from the publisher. Requests for photocopying of any part of this book shall be directed in writing to Access Copyright, 1 Yonge Street, Suite 1900, Toronto, Ontario, M5E 1E5.

National Library of Canada Cataloguing in Publication

Safarik, Allan, 1948-
Blood of angels / Allan Safarik.

Poems.
ISBN 1-894345-68-1

I. Title.

PS8587.A245B56 2004   C811'.54   C2004-900863-3

Cover photograph, *Market Garden, St. Peter's, 7:00 a.m.* by Don Hall
Cover and book design by J. Forrie
Typeset by Thistledown Press Ltd.
Printed and bound in Canada

Thistledown Press Ltd.
633 Main Street
Saskatoon, Saskatchewan, S7H 0J8
www.thistledown.sk.ca

Thistledown Press gratefully acknowledges the financial assistance of the Canada Council for the Arts, the Saskatchewan Arts Board, and the Government of Canada through the Book Publishing Industry Development Program for its publishing program.

NOTE

During 1999-2000, the author was the Writer-in-Residence in Humboldt and District, Saskatchewan. He was able to find weekly refuge at Severin Hall at St Peter's Abbey in Muenster, 10 kilometres down the road from downtown Humboldt. These poems were written in the winter and spring following the residency.

With gratitude to citizens in the Humboldt District and to the Benedictines and others in the community at St Peter's Abbey and College, a spiritual haven for writers. These poems are purely serendipitous, based incidentally on the living, without malice or aforethought. With thanks to Dolores Reimer for interesting insights and to the Saskatchewan Writers' Guild programs and the Saskatchewan Arts Board for a grant that allowed me time to complete this manuscript.

"Sanctuary", "First Winter Storm", and "Witness" were first published in *Listening with the Ear of the Heart* (St. Peter's Press, 2002).

Books are a collaborative effort. Thanks to Don Hall for the cover photo and to Seán Virgo, a thought provoking editor.

CONTENTS

THE HARVEST OF SOULS

10	The Sowing
11	Dream About It
12	Blood Of Angels
13	What Freedom Hath The Hour?
14	From *Holy Ladder*
15	Martyrs
16	The Dog's Black Lips
17	Probable Scenario
18	Sanctuary
19	Visitor
20	The Angel Plays Chess Badly
21	The Brothers Trade In Their Cassocks For Cashmere Sweaters
25	In The Movie Of The Moment
26	An Angel Tours By Bus
27	The Harvest Of Souls
29	Nocturne
30	Night Walker
31	Outside In
32	New Year's Resolution: St Peter's Abbey
33	After The Angel

THE HOLY ROAD

36	The Holy City
37	Meeting The Apostles On The Road To Heaven
38	The Grave
39	Let Us Find Out Who Among Us
40	Messenger
41	Dangerous Not To Believe
42	Antioch
44	Storyteller
45	Magician
46	The Holy Road
47	Like Napoleon Leaving Russia
49	Cargo
52	Siege
53	What Tree Will Make The Cross?

54	Fleas
55	Portrait Of Truce In The Twentieth Century
56	Elegy For A Slain Archbishop
58	Hard Rain
60	The Execution
62	Prayer For The Newborn Martyr
63	Things That Might Have Been
64	If I Remain Here
65	Exile
66	The Traveller At the Beginning And End Of Time
67	Winter's Tale

ABBEY MEDITATIONS

70	*Invocation*
71	*Prologue*
72	Faith
73	Under The Apricot Moon
74	Butterfly Wing
75	The Roots Of Piety
76	Meditation On An Empty Pail
77	Bitter Wind On Fall Trees
78	For He Who Finds Fault
79	Night Of Brawny Stars
80	October Song
81	Shelter Belt
82	Scarecrow
83	Dialogue
84	First Winter Storm
85	Anchorite
86	Deliverance
87	Witness
88	Onion Skins
89	Winter Epilogue
90	Dear Brother Of God
91	But Then Who Am I To Say
93	Praise The Quiet Sky
94	Hymn For The Last One Left On Earth
95	*Epilogue*

In memory of Robert Safarik
1971 – 2001

the HARVEST of Souls

THE SOWING

Miracles are not easily discouraged
God sees to that, in a transparent world
the sun and moon divide the day in half;
the light and the absence of light
Ancient process born in the heavens
the order of all things humble and beloved
Warm sun on the earth, cold water thirst
Wind shaking laughter in the trees

The crippled sage working in his garden
among the tender green beginnings of another season
digs in the fresh turned earth with his bare hands
I think he might be a dirty angel in disguise
Lucky to be alive after the harsh winter or
a mere intruder in the transitory illusion
The double white peony opens its flower
Summer days sleep in the deepening shade
Drowsy bumblebees fly up
from a small opening in the ground
Hidden bird on the hillside sings a faint persistent song
A white cabbage butterfly lands on a dark green vine

Later in the evening in search of a destination
Headlights deep in blue flowers
the car lurches across an uneven field
At the edge of the deep coulee a falling star
vanishing into the dark emptiness
marks the beginning of another moment
These were the things I was thinking about
After all that has been done and thought of,
life turning lonely and small, depends
on a handful of dried seeds planted in time

DREAM ABOUT IT

Salvador Dali's face
in the bath-
room mirror
all steamed up
from my
shower

long shoe-
lace moustache
a hovering
swarm
of fruit flies
below olive
black
hooded
Spanish eyes

I erase him
with a wet towel
but his face
lingers in the
drops
of steam

after I am
dressed
ready
to go out
I find
a cricket
in my shoe

BLOOD OF ANGELS

Black and white kitty
preening outside
the kitchen door
one opaque eye
in a quizzical face
hairless scars
running the length
of its thin back
as if it escaped
from a skinning
machine
or a maniac with
a filleting knife

Blood red
underneath white
grey-fringed clouds
evening piling up
in the western sky
sun peering above
the horizon like
a half-cooked egg

I sit down
on the hard bench
put my hand
tentatively
on its head
it purrs, rubbing
against my leg
songs of birds
nesting
in the chimneys
light dying
on the tin roof

WHAT FREEDOM HATH THE HOUR!

A hermit who lived a long time in the shadow
of a huge tree came out in the sun. He had been
so busy with his tasks and his contemplations that
he was astonished to see the tree he planted from
a sapling so many decades before had matured
into a stately shade tree. This dose of reality gave
the hermit cause to consider his quest completed

He sent a note to the Abbott seeking permission
to return to the daily routine of the order.
The hermit in humble words felt he had achieved
his greater goal of living in the light of God's love.
His concentration had been of such depth
that he took the immense shade for granted,
thus showing the intensity of his devotion

The Abbott denied his request but sent him a saw
Brother, he wrote, Cut down your pride.
Devotion cannot be measured by a monument.
When you finish sawing, chop it into cords and
stack it on the leeward side of the hedge.
Notice how the shade turns into sweat.
Think of the pleasure you bring my hearth's fire

FROM *HOLY LADDER*

*When for some reason
I was sitting outside a monastery,
near the cells of those living in solitude,
I heard them fighting by themselves
in their cells like caged partridges
from bitterness and anger,
leaping at the face of their offender
as if he were actually present.*

*I devoutly advised them
not to stay in solitude in case
they should be changed
from human beings into demons.*

*One could see how the tongues
of some of them were parched
and hung out of their mouths like dogs'.
Some chastised themselves in the scorching sun,
others tormented themselves in the cold.*

*Some, having tasted a little water
so as not to die of thirst, stopped drinking;
others, having nibbled a little bread,
flung the rest of it away, and said that
they were unworthy of being fed
like human beings, since they had
behaved like beasts*

— Found in the writings of St. John Climacus,
Abbot at the Monastery of Sinai, sixth century

MARTYRS

They grow
in the fields,
upright men
Bright green
arms raised to
the blazing sun

Birds jump
among them
splattering
bloody drops
on straw mulch

When dry
and withered
they are snipped
off close to
the ground

THE DOG'S BLACK LIPS

Growing from rich ground,
the tulip's black petals shine in the light
Rain falls gently in the morning
The wheelbarrow leaves its mark
across the manicured lawn
The gardener's footprints
sluff along behind like brackets
around a piece of printed text

When birds stop singing
darkness creeps over the eyes
Thoughts beautiful as spring
flowers begin to die *en masse*
Blood in the throat runs cold
flesh turns the colour of ivory
The panting dog's pink tongue
lolling from black lips
announces the coming of angels

PROBABLE SCENARIO

My ex discussing
ecclesiastic law with the Pope
while they sip dry red wine
and eat prosciutto and
portebello mushrooms
In the meantime, she
remembers to speak
to him about moving
St Francis of Assisi
into a more prominent
position since he looks
out of place parked
behind the flowers
in the outer foyer

The Pope gives her
a benign smile which
she answers in kind
and tells her it takes
centuries to decide
the smallest detail
but for her anything's
possible, picking
up the phone
he orders it be done

In the afternoon
she returns from
her little walk
in the fields
near Muenster
gathering dead weeds,
ancient stones
A wreath of white
bent-winged birds
circle overhead

SANCTUARY

Two monks with stooped backs,
Shuffling feet, walk in the afternoon
Brittle as dried plants in arid soil
they can barely move against
the slight breeze that ruffles
thin white hair and scruffy beards
Together they have been on duty
serving God for a hundred years

They bear the signs of a long siege
Years have fallen before them
in dim rooms and quiet enclaves
Oppressed by the virtue of solitude
the mind grows a long vegetable
Celery green with pale yellow
blossoms and scraggy brown
roots in the deeper loam

VISITOR

If only the words
of your speaking
cease in time

the cat walks
imperious
from the room
tail held high
like a signal
or judgement
from above

I motion with
my hand, pray
continue
talking,
I know
no way
to stop
the future
in your eyes

those who die
forsaken,
unafraid
scare me
silent

THE ANGEL PLAYS CHESS BADLY

Angel of unknown origin, except the obvious:
Sent by God, large white unmanageable wings
that project from her back like a hide-a-bed
when she takes off her unfashionable raincoat.
And dogs, even small insignificant lap dogs,
minus their gonads, try hard to intimidate
with their yappy little opera-singer voices
until she preens and folds the feathers
around her thin-waisted girlish figure
After dinner she inquired about a smoking room
A few of the brothers were a little surprised
that God hadn't cured her of the habit
Turned out she was a non-smoker
but figured all the interesting sinners
would be puffing away in the games room

The Hungarian was savouring a Dutch cigar
that came in a metal box with a picture
of a leopard looking rather bored
A bit down on his luck, he's not here because
he's spiritual but for the cheap room and meal
When she barged in she caught her wing
over the doorjamb, spilling her coffee on the rug
"Perhaps, you'd care for a game of chess,"
she remarked, "or how about a game of eight ball?"
"No," he said, "I don't play supernaturals."
"Surely you can see, I'm just new at the job."
"Yeh," his face tightened like a fox,"they all say that.
But I'll play Russian Roulette in the back of my car
or shoot an apple off your head with a crossbow.
If I win, he'll just send another in your place."

THE BROTHERS TRADE IN THEIR CASSOCKS FOR CASHMERE SWEATERS

The movie crowd arrived
at Muenster in August
to make a sweet little film
about faith and contemplation
I imagine brothers walking about
in Pierre Cardin sweaters
While corn pops in the fields
the sun pours butter
on the precise landscape
The pretend Abbot
in the picture's background
wearing the Russian sable hat
challenges all comers
to a game of darts

A thousand guests
have come from afar
for the u-pick strawberries
The bells are pealing off
old Beatle tunes,
just now a head banging
version of "Hey Jude"
Can you envision
turning me loose
in a place like this?
Three times a day
the camel passes
through the eye
of the needle

I stand in my
yellow trunks
wearing a Mae West,
yelling, "Surf's up"
The maraca players
and the steel guitar
band start up

Too soon clouds gather
rumbling thunder rolls by
Everybody goes inside
to play Scrabble and shoot pool
while the cooling rain
good for smiling flowers
ruins the orgami passion play
in the courtyard
By four o'clock the sun has dried
everything back to normal
The Cinzano beach umbrellas go
scurrying off in the wind
colourful crepe paper ribbons
stream behind like kite tails
whipping at the sky
over the ultra green lawn

Trees are shaking lovely fronds
to Caribbean rhythms
One time in the new
millennium only,
Carnivali Benedicto!

When Jesus came out
already mounted on the cross
I understood the nature
of my slobbering daydreamscape
The secret was, I couldn't tell
the actors from the monks
after a while I begin to believe
the monks couldn't either

Movie cameras rolled
until the director yelled, "Cut!"
The make-up artist

knew the difference
hitting certain faces
with her powdery pompoms

The smallish monk
in the black robe,
a famous Quebecois actor,
smooths his tonsure in place
with an abalone
inlaid brush
checking every detail
in an oval hand mirror
Cute as an oyster
in the shell
it snapped shut
with a vengeance

The fly waking me
from the sleep of death
with his buzzing attacks
flew around for a while
before he landed
on the slice
of sacred lemon pie
that I smuggled in from
the glorious afternoon
blessed by bees, dragonflies,
bluebottles and grubs

Suddenly when
I felt footsteps
walking above me
I realized that I traded in
my room for a coffin
in an ancient cemetery
with quaint garden
decorations and yellow cedars

Liberace, grinning wildly
in the background
plays the devotional
hymns of the ages
on the pipe organ
A quiet voice on the surface
reads names, date,
and inscriptions

IN THE MOVIE OF THE MOMENT

White clouds break up overhead
the director of *Solitude* talks into a head set
to the cameraman moving down the track
The actors look casually detached before
they commit intimate acts with the camera
The dialogue is recorded softly
into the machine so that bystanders
can hear nothing but equipment hum

The end of every scene like *ego-interruptus*
as the players sag back into their true selves
A few go outside and throw a frisbee, another
stays nearby, weeping in the rose garden
Some bystanders want to get autographs
but sense it isn't the right time to pounce,
others surge forward on uncertain ground
holding out their scraps of lined paper

AN ANGEL TOURS BY BUS

Summer's flowers near the end
haphazard in their beds
petals strewn around by wind
A ragged bee touches down
on a wounded bloom, all shot to hell
by withering months of heat
and slashing wind
sex-starved insects hump
on the eyelid of the sun

Saddened by the bell
clanging in the foreground
calling everyone to prayer
I pack my cardboard box
and walk one last time past
the walls of blue spruce trees
that line the abbey streets
Watch my shadow grow so small
it disappears into the hand-
kerchief when I blow my nose

Somewhere destiny in a top hat
carrying a 44 magnum is waiting for
someone coming home from
a long night's journey to paradise
I've been on the bus before
there's no place to go back to
better than where I'm going
The garden dying back
I pin a butterfly to my lapel

After all this time, the sun
still waits on the open highway
When I pull the shade down
on the black night
I'll be two hundred miles
in the future travelling
in style across the universe

HARVEST OF SOULS

The souls are growing under the fields
The souls are pushing their heads through to the sun
The souls are new and green and fresh as lime juice
sleeping in the afternoon heat
begging for flowing water
leaning away from the wind
are turning a copper colour
The souls are lush and ready for harvest
dug like new potatoes
threshed like spring wheat
The souls are filled with sweet nectar
are buzzing among the flowers
The souls are gourds and plums and beans
The souls are ripe and ready to pick

The souls are wearing coats of dust
The souls are hiding in the underbrush
treading water in the well
singing in the darkness
burning in the night
The souls are banished by thunder
The souls are praying in the wilderness
wishing for divine mercy
deafened by pealing bells
The souls are caged birds in the basement
The souls are shadows in the cathedral
are mortar between the bricks
are voices listening in the pews
The souls are trapped in stained-glass windows

The souls are overdrawn at the bank
are going on a long vacation
are checking into a cheap motel
are playing games of chance

The souls are sunning themselves on the beach
are showing off their new tattoos
are romancing strangers in the afternoons
The souls are passing bad cheques in dingy bars
The souls are dancing on the table tops
drunk on gallons of cheap wine
plucking feathers from an angel
The souls are waiting on the hands of time
The souls are in possession of one-way bus tickets
The souls are never sure they're coming back

The souls are lost in the rain clouds
are soaring in the windy sky
ragged, tattered and torn
hanging in tree limbs
are shrieking like old hags
The souls are white and red and black and green
are voices in the inky universe
are water lapping the edges
The souls are flocking up to go south
The souls are ancestors whispering in the trees
The souls are vanishing into the bloody sunset

NOCTURNE

The candle
flame sways in
the breeze

I touch
my fingers
to my lips

Gently
blow it out,
exhaling

Sorry, there's
no place
to hide

Even behind
brick walls,
black robes

NIGHT WALKER

Lonely nights in a big inky well of muddled stars
I walked along the edges of the bright yellow field
felt the wind shaking the trees with a heavy hand
Hoping Van Gogh might show up one night
and give these monks a run for their spiritual selves
but mostly only pitiful travellers
some needing bus tickets to far places
Others, wanting to exchange useless lives
for lives of substance, usually manage to stay
a week before vanishing on the highway
the white geese came and stayed in the fields for months

Cold tunnels of brick and stone
worn smooth from seven generations
By the end of the year I mastered
the steps in the darkened stairwells
How do you cope with the energy from all that praying?
Like an after-effect, the gurgle of water rushes
into the parched garden. Voices do the same
The worshiping sun transfixes the cornfield
The word of God transfixes the cathedral
Outside the grass grows lush
under the bellies of waddling geese

OUTSIDE IN

Get up from your knees brother
If only you could look into the future
You'll be there in the corner of the room
for many decades to come
Blue and white flowers
small heart-shaped leaves among
wet stones on the winding path
Finally, reaching the edge of the wall
you turn back to the ordinary way
of being perceived in the community
Your lack of discipline called into question
Birds singing intermittently along
the trail tell you about it

Lost your alien habits in the transformation
Time hangs on you like a winter coat
Sunlight flickers through rustling leaves
Now they know what you're thinking
it will keep you humble and repentant
Go back to your prayers, good brother
The other dimension you think about
dwells only in the self
Delicate white pea flowers
hover in the windy garden
Tendrils curl around the wire
The sun breaks through the window
on brilliant spokes of broken light

NEW YEAR'S RESOLUTION: ST. PETER'S ABBEY

Massaging my legs, cold as ivory, twice as white
in the middle of star-spangled winter
I got up and went next door to the smoking room
Put out a small piece of blue cheese for the mouse
Watched him run with his smelly burden
along the baseboard to the end of the wall
and down the crevice into the foundation
Must remember to build him a tiny shopping cart
to make his life easier in the coming year

I was thinking about the *Bird Man of Alcatraz*
How easy it would be for me, in my undershirt,
looking a little like Burt Lancaster,
to become the Mouse Man of Muenster
Chewing the nutritious mixture of cream
and whole grain bread into a thick pap
before I feed the naked baby mice
with an eyedropper from the monk's infirmary
Knitting them little suits from cat hair wool
I have spun on my tiny spinning wheel
I keep hidden under the mattress

When the warden called me into his office
for a little chat about my activities
I refused to cooperate but still manage to drink
the bowl of tomato soup and put the cellophane
wrapped soda crackers into my shirt pocket for later
A treat I'll crush and scatter for my friends
"Is it true," he asks, twisting his Pat O'Brian
face into a calm fatherly version of authority,
"that you've gone soft in your old age?
It won't matter, you'll never get out alive."

AFTER THE ANGEL

Wind scraping hard across the stubble field
Found your footsteps just before dark
Warmed my hands on a candle stub
Turned my head to listen to the stars
hissing like neon lights in the icy sky

Stared through the empty wilderness
Wandered far into the ethereal world
the dream came apart in my mind
Still here locked in the moment
fly buzzing around the hot metal fixture

Let the phone ring its warning all night
Decided not to listen to smug goodbyes
Former friends gone south for the rest of time
It got lonely in the future except for the
sound of the tap dripping its message

Gone for good it said, even a blind man
could see that, if he tried imagining
God's icy fingers grasping his face
while the fire in his soul burns down
to glimmer at him in the darkened place

the HOLY Road

THE HOLY CITY

The pilgrim returns to the holy city
Where death waits on every street corner
His prayers are stronger than his fears
Even then, the fig merchants warn of disaster
Bus stations are empty of people
but for workers who are too poor to matter
and the stream of pilgrims who accept
God's wisdom and divine protection
The water seller is nervous in the heat of the day
His shiny cups tinkle like bells as he walks away
warning the American tourists not to take his picture
The police following, quickly pick him up
spilling his goat skin in the unslakeable dust
Pigeons strut around in the square
Iridescent neck feathers squint at the sun

The pilgrim returns to his cheap shelter
He is wearing loose white clothing and sandals
He is a vegetarian who drinks bottled water
In the middle of the night when they come for him
he has already gone into the hills with a shepherd
The waterseller is dying on a meat hook
in the police station basement where his cries
are heard by all the citizens in the neighborhood
He has already confessed to being guilty of everything
It is the custom for traitors and villains to expire
slowly in the hands of the secret police
Eventually, they tire of his confessions
and butcher him like an animal for the market
In the morning the white city shimmers
in heat mirages, kites circle overhead

MEETING THE APOSTLES ON THE ROAD TO HEAVEN

The poets are here,
walking past the hedges
on the hard packed roadway
Passing the paper cornfield
on their way back from the cemetery
I can hear their feet crunch
on the gravel and the hesitant
nervous gasoline laughter
poured onto the words
before they stop
and light the match.
Not in grace I pass by

Small grey birds the monks
have taught to walk
on their arms and shoulders
for a hundred generations
flutter down from spruce branches
and hover over tiny snow
flake crumbs melting
in my palms

Suddenly
after a long silence
the sky blows up
in my face

THE GRAVE

Pity the man without faith
half-starved, brutalized
digging his own grave
in wasted ground
while joking soldiers
passing a bottle
of whiskey around
stamp their feet
impatiently

If he was home
he'd make a pot of soup
and climb into his cozy bed
When he hits hard pan
the sound of the shovel
scraping the earth stops

Cold sun dancing
on his neck tickles like
a spider in the dark
Drops of sweat freeze
on lips mumbling
the shovel is my voice
Warming his hands
with his last few breaths
children's faces flash by

A single shot
echoes over the flats
a thousand white geese
feeding in the pea fields
jump, honking and gabbling
into the hole in the sky

LET US FIND OUT WHO AMONG US

Every man
tempted
by the weakness
in every
other man
The mob
hangs the
innocents
in the crotch
of a tree

There are no
exemptions
for body
language
or clever
personality

A few try
to buy
their way out
others begging
for mercy
simply
go crazy
before the end
Some turn
to prayer

Until the
manila
rope tightens
around
your neck
How will
you tell
if you're
dreaming?

THE MESSENGER

Came quietly and humbly to the back door
Delivered his message while he devoured
a loaf of bread and ate two helpings of stew
His eyes never looked up or made contact
He traded his watch for a used pair of boots
before he left the ancient city and now
he is wrapping a sandwich to eat later
before he reaches the border crossing

In mid-morning when they released the sewage
several headless bodies floated down the river
"Tomorrow they will begin slaughtering
monks, nuns and true believers until the river
turns the colour of blood, unless everything
in the name of God burns to the ground."
He made the sign of the cross before
wiping greasy fingers on his shirt front

When he left under the cover of darkness
the dogs in the yard rushed at him barking
hysterically until the whites of their eyes bulged
Men in the shadows with hands on their knives
watched as he grew smaller in the murk
By the evening it became apparent the candle
stick holders were missing from the church
At midnight fires burned half way to the horizon

DANGEROUS NOT TO BELIEVE

Men in the streets wore the same coats
cut from the same bolts of cloth
They drank in the same taverns
sang the same patriotic songs
ate the same food at the same places
Their children went to the same schools
played in the same parks on the same teams
They got married and buried in the same church
where they prayed to the same God

Prudent to swallow the party line
The priest stopped in the street
looked over his glasses and asked
Why you weren't coming to confession
When the barber put the razor
on your throat and demanded the truth,
bluffing to save your life you said:
"Shave it close as you can," while the
lying pores on your neck swelled up like peas

ANTIOCH

impossible to remember all the names
of conquering heroes written in gold
carved in relief on ornate balconies
only time travelled unobstructed
through the green mountain pass across
stony land to the edge of the mirage
where crusaders marched before
the masters of the hunting falcon

godly men, unhappy in territory, sent out armies
to conquer unbeliever souls unwashed
unholy under the silence of the fiery sun
repent or perish in the purifying flames!
pike men thick as a forest came ashore
with hunting dogs and human coursers
priests and friars, lords, and temple buyers
craving gold and slaves and souls to save

god shining on massed breastplates and silver
helmets reflect the hacking blades of death
god of resplendent mounted kings
outside unholy temples speaking holy words
from the body of spiritual language
god of the catapult and the longbow
god of the hammer in righteous hands
pounding demons from the nomad's skull

time flees the mirage of broken dreams
filling the horizon with bloodshed and chaos
great wallowing warhorses screaming in pain
from the immense heat blown into frothy lungs
died slowly in their own bubbling foam
scimitars drawn across their masters' throats
the looted baggage train scattered over
wavy sand dunes risen like the tide

bones galore under sun-blasted sand
in the dry blood bed of satiated desire
the sword drank like a thirsty dog and
vultures gorged from dung heaps
beneath thinly veiled desert stars
under the gleaned bones of the universe
mullahs drank mint tea in billowing pavilions
indifferent camels grazed the acacias

STORYTELLER

Two fingers torn out,
the beautifully flawed hand nearly
always out of sight
hiding in a pocket or being
embraced by its mate

This was the way it went,
until the torturer heard the truth
now it shakes every hand
offered as if the hand of God
on judgment day

MAGICIAN

the white rabbit
disappears in green sun-
light without trace

three shiny crows
with split tongues
drown in the dust

the amateur wives
of holy men
rest in the shade

THE HOLY ROAD

Every night he bathed the injured leg
in salt and herbs trying to cure the wound
but it only grew larger turning yellow in the bone
Now he limps home to the turnip supper
and the mandatory glass of grog
The dogs yip and bark, the gates close

Everything will be resolved this summer
The outsiders are watching on the hill
Yesterday they poisoned the water holes
The sheep are already rotting in the valley
At night their fires burn like eyes among the stars
In the flickering oil of midnight light
he sharpens the rust from his blade

This war never really starts or ends
but like all wars simmers forever on the
hearths of storytellers and old scarred men
The woman and children have gone
into the underground caves by the river
The priests have buried the golden idols

Tomorrow he will limp down the dusty road
on his way to the communal garden
stopping before he reaches the perimeter fence
to announce his arrival with a pocket mirror
When he gets the signal to come ahead
he will find the severed heads
of his tribe mounted on the pickets

LIKE NAPOLEON LEAVING RUSSIA

On December 5th, 1812 Napoleon handed over supreme command to Murat. On the night of December 18, at full gallop the Emperor's carriage bore him through the Arc de Triomphe and as the clock struck the last quarter before midnight he alighted safe and sound at the central entrance of the Tuileries.
— JFC Fuller

The sounds of thousands of horses
and men dying in the gore of Beresina
echoing in the bloody wasteland below
pungent grey clouds of cannon smoke
Frozen, broken, half-dead army stragglers
in their thousands plunging into snowy fields
Knives of death pulled hard across
the bare throats of the nearly-done-in
by the ghostly fingers of invisible mercy
The newly dying twisted in grotesque postures
Angels of God pulling out their souls
freeing them over the icy plains

Napoleon rushes ahead so he can spare
his eyes from witnessing the aftermath,
After three days march the Emperor's Guard
stand down for a day of rest while
Napoleon sleeps off his miserable mood
As always, he dreams of impossible victories
against the conquering armies of mankind
throughout the centuries, waking up refreshed
by the power and glory of his own greatness

He fires up his officers with an inspiring speech
about turning adversity into advantage

In the middle of his talk he craves an egg
but nobody has seen a chicken for months
It is a simple problem that turns him rigid
and he rages about the incompetence
that is rampant in the Grand Army
He sits down at his portable writing desk and
orders the generals make him a breakfast omelet
To make matters worse the band is too frozen up
to play his favourite marching tunes

Finally, a chicken is located but alas, it's a rooster
and the Emperor is not in the mood for *coq au vin*
The bird, unaware it's living on borrowed time
struts around the cooking fires showing off
its shimmering neck feathers while Bonaparte
sends dispatches to the supply office
requisitioning fresh eggs for the officers' mess
He is famous for taking care of every little detail
In the next few months, when he begins
recruiting a new army, he'll be philosophical
about his time spent in Russia
Four hundred and fifty thousand French corpses
left behind to fertilize the steppes

CARGO

Ship's lanterns torch the rippled sea
Wind illustrating waves with yellow
calligraphy on blue/green water
A sailing ship from another century
makes its way along the coastline
infrequently sending a landing party
ashore for fresh water and meat
They leave a marker and stake
a claim in a formal ceremony
with God as their witness
while they placate the locals
with colourful trinkets and beads

From a misty fiord long canoes loaded
with crones come alongside
The chaplain tries to communicate
by pointing upward and waving
his crucifix over their heads
while saying the *Lord's Prayer*
This causes the ancient hags
to wave their arms wildly
The captain below decks
drunk and sick from Portuguese brandy
will soon be dead from the hole
that has opened up in his guts

The women climbing onboard
have been reaching for and pointing
at the sailors' bulging crotches
Soon the mate and the crew are
fornicating with them on the deck
Old dry crones, surprisingly spry
passionately roll their eyes and move
their hips vigorously to the task at hand
while the seamen plod at it

like the big horses in the
breeding sheds at home

When the kegs of rum arrived
passed on hand over hand
from the bowels of the vessel
the party turned for the worst
The dangling hags were half-
strangled and mutilated
in the rigging before they were cut
down and thrown overboard

On a three month journey
becalmed for five weeks
in the Horse Latitudes
by a glassy windless sea
The long grey torpid shadow
under the ship's hull has had
only two chickens and the ship's cat
that fell from the rigging
to vary its diet of garbage
and human waste

Now the scuppers are awash
streams of blood flow into the sea
Shark, swimming in frothy gore
attacks the thrashing limbs
body parts strewn about like bait fish
In another few days after some
last inspirational words the big fish
will have the captain in his canvas shroud
before he can slide down
through the choppy waves
on the cannon ball's weight

Below decks, twenty Carmelite nuns
bound for a mission in the New World
are on their knees praying
for deliverance from the voyage
that sailed off the edge of the world
into the burgundy sea
of hell and damnation

Praying for deliverance:
From the terror of men's buttocks
in their frenzied work
and their rivers of hairy sweat
From the screams and groans
of betrayed lovers
butchered and thrown
into the Devil's teeth
From the horror and power
of God's primitive witness,
Leviathan, bumping the hull
From the sound of holystones
scouring the deck
and the innocent voices
of early morning song

SIEGE

The siege engine failed dislodging
the inhabitants who have burrowed
into the mountainside
Nothing to do but wait outside
until they starve to death
Three years pass, every morning
they stand naked on the parapets
bending away from our direction

The King says we must not fail
to put them all to a fiery death
for their lack of faith in the old Gods
and their failure to fear his sword
The priest thinks the winter months,
when the rains fall and the desert blooms,
will bring a great victory
He holds fire in his hands and sees
many skeletons dancing in flames

The King who also speaks
to the Gods binds the priest in chains
and locks him in a cage
with an unfed carrion eater
"Charlatan, I will believe you
unless the filthy bird of truth
puts out your lying eyes"

WHICH TREE WILL MAKE THE CROSS?

Tree of life growing on the hill top
Mile post, marker of time and distance
Great canopy of shelter from the storm

Which man will hammer in the nails
Leave him crucified in the bloody street
Will it be labourer, soldier or priest?

FLEAS

In the summer of the holiest feast
old clothes, straw beds were burned
fleas became an element of dust
In the dark fields of eternity
a city was besieged by armies of stars

Fleas from the body of Christ
lived through centuries
hiding in hair, feeding on human blood
Cloth smoldered, straw beds withered
When he died there on the cross
fleas gave up the ship
dropping onto Roman soldiers
who paused on the road to stare
The stars went on glittering
with cricket sounds
Citizens of Rome were infested
by ravaging hordes of biting fleas
Even those wearing the finest
Cathay silk were not immune

All the Roman deities nearly scratched
themselves to death, slaves rejoiced
seeing gods turning into mortals
standing with senators and whores
beside the heaping pyres of rosewood

PORTRAIT OF TRUCE IN THE TWENTIETH CENTURY

A white flag ripped
from a dead man's shroud
droops in the blue haze
over flooded trenches
Both sides are out
in no-mans-land
picking up corpses
On days like this
human beings
think that God has
abandoned them in
the Devil's headquarters

The two-foot soldiers
in the lower foreground
locked in a timeless frame
in a photographic instant
Bewildered eyes stare
hard into the future
This time the camera's
an honest witness
The dead man's
knuckles bounce over
uneven ground

ELEGY FOR A SLAIN ARCHBISHOP
In memory of Archbishop Oscar Arnulfo Romero

Blood in the beautiful blonde hair
of *el presidente*'s youthful consort
blood on her dreadfully gashed lips
almost bitten off by the passionate beast
blood on his chauffeur's white gloves
stuffed down her pretty throat

A hand puts a gun to a head
and fires a slug into the sunshine
between a man's eyes while he's
reading his newspaper
in a boulevard café
everybody stays down
on the floor for five minutes
a procedure the authorities recommend
to enhance the chances of long life
the sun beats against the bloody
Rorschach blot on the adobe wall
once again the only witness is dead

The horror of truth slaughtered
everyday on newscasts
vivid mental pictures
soaking up newspaper pages
blood on the hands
of the investigators,
the doctors, the coroners,
the generals, the ministers
of church and state

Archbishop Romero's blood
in the laundry of the ruling class
in the homes of the assassins
their friends, families, countrymen

in their nurseries smeared
on their immaculate babies

Archbishop Romero's blood
in their waste buckets
in their white kitchen pails,
dripping in their bathroom sinks,
around the old urinals
in the football parks
bloody fingerprints
on the golden faucets
in the country clubs

Martyr's blood
puddling in daydreams
and in sleep
the blood, the blood
never stops flowing
on cathedral stairs,
or in the streets

— On March 24, 1980, while celebrating the Eucharist, Archbishop Romero of El Salvador was shot and killed at the altar by a death-squad assassin.

HARD RAIN

Low land where fresh
water meets salty
When the sea comes in
flowing over the marsh
the sun reflects the sky
in the watery bed
When the tide goes out
red-throated birds peck
at black mud the colour
of their feathers

Rumours of war are everywhere
Armies march in the night
By morning they are massed
at the border awaiting orders
All at once the new immigrants
waiting to get in have a ready
market for their wares
The radio warns the troops
on various health issues

Traffic police in both countries
are out in force on their bicycles
trying to straighten out the
confusion of tanks,
some have been impounded
for being double parked
in front of beer halls

The Latin teacher cancels
his classes to make it easier
on the students who have
the farthest to travel,
in case the buses
stop running

At the castle a pair of swans
are mating in the bullrushes
that ring the moat
No shade of green
in the fern grottoes
in all of Christendom
as subtle to the eye
as the widowed Queen's
sacred ancestral shroud
that has been blessed
for centuries by
wandering sarabaites

In the afternoon while
the garden's being planted
for the seven hundred
and fiftieth season
in succession
a worker discovers
a one ton bomb
buried beneath
the gazebo

THE EXECUTION

The general came outside
to witness the execution
This was unusual since
he seldom took a personal
interest in such matters
The visiting foreign priests
on either side of him
on the presidential carpet
chatted about purely
secular affairs

When the Captain
of the Guard approached
with the blindfold
he whipped out a good cigar
placed it into the prisoner's
mouth lighting it boldly
with one stroke
of the wooden match
on the crease
in his uniform pants

When the captain
lowered his arm
the guns fired in unison
Viewed through
cloying blue smoke
the prisoner slumped
against his bounds
as if reposing
in a lawn chair

The general retires
into the shade behind
the viewing stand
with his profitable friends

to enjoy a double brandy
and picnic on sauteed squab
He doesn't know his visitors
disguised as priests
have already collected
many gold bars

When they stop laughing
at the general's jokes
his guests offered
to conjure an illusion
for his entertainment
They levitated him
over the banquet table
before they cut his throat
with a straight razor

The general's life
ran quickly through
his manicured hands
irrefutable evidence
of absolute surprise
and proof of death
in one swift act
He remained unblinking
and docile as a lamb

When they stuffed
the burning cigar
between his fat lips
smoke poured
from the gaping hole
They did such a good
job he couldn't speak
his eyes said it all

PRAYER FOR THE NEWBORN MARTYR

Coming into the world on a lousy afternoon
Snowing in city streets, the highway out is closed
Stores are shutting early, buses have stopped running
muzzled winter steaming from ventilation systems
lingers in the alleys and on boulevards
The homeless man settles down to a hard sleep
there's a broken whiskey bottle on the pavement
A dead pigeon falls from the tenement ledge
cockroaches scamper on the wallpaper
beside the hot plate on the bedstead
By 6 pm the heat has been turned off
just in time for your arrival and the guns
have started shelling the city again

They took you home in a crocheted blanket
wrapped up against the scourge of weather
The bright red marks on your head
blood of your own being close to the skin
You take your nourishment on the run
escaping the fires burning in the rubble
God loves you as much as his own son
the priest says baptizing you with holy water

Going away from the world on a lousy afternoon
The same way you came in from the cold
Nearly half a century gone like a dream
Nothing to believe in if you are afraid to die
Think you can sit in the dark waiting
for the mechanical hands winding down
increments of time inside a metal jacket
Will God be there when you need him?

Traffic piled up on icy freeway lanes
Power lines down in the industrial section
Trains have stopped running in the country
with blizzards closing down commuter lines
Waited too long for the message that didn't come
your killers are already slinking up the backstairs

THINGS THAT MIGHT HAVE BEEN

Sun breaks across the serpent sky
in the dawn of the Ganges
white birds rise up in a heat mirage
a cortege wreathed in marigolds floats by
carrying the body of death wrapped in a shroud
What can stop me from dreaming
about places I've never been?

Carved elephant doorways
fragrant oranges in shaded grottoes
severed monkey hands in the bazaar
grey-headed nuns washing bodies
a gaunt dog eating its own feces

the amputated daughter holding up her tin cup
So many little dyings, it doesn't matter
which one might be real

IF I REMAIN HERE

Sunlight on faded walls
before the window shade
can block it entering the room

I left a little bloody pool in the sink
where I shaved my throat,
word is out in the morning

When they come for me
I know you'll be there
quietly reassuring my children
it's all a mistake

EXILE

white limitless prairie, a plate illustrated by
a severe, disciplined hand
steel pen etched in the reflected glare
window glass at forty below
ribbon of smoke rushing out from brick walls
draped over the trees
sulphuric acid bites into the metal
like a voracious reptile
the small figure in the distance, coming back
against the wind,
anonymous in the landscape, walks right
through the picture

THE TRAVELLER AT THE BEGINNING AND END OF TIME

As you set out for the frontier the government stops you
and requests your appearance at a show trial
for unbelievers who have defied the edicts of old men

Before you are through testifying as to your innocence
hundreds will have been processed in the basement
by a bloodthirsty chorus of professional sadists

One after another citizens come before the magistrates
with broken bones and sprained limbs
summarily sentenced to afterlife
in a mass grave buried below the waterline

Engineers have already started to drain the canal
bureaucrats assign relatives of the doomed to slave ships

Before the day is out the authorities decide you
a simple commercial traveller know nothing
about politics or the workings of the state

In the climate of the times you can understand
how no one is above suspicion or reproach

That the letting of blood is a necessary purging
and you unfortunately are no longer free to go abroad
because of the awful things you have witnessed

They will be merciful blinding you with a sharpened stick
to keep you a beggar beholding of their good will
and help you forget what you have memorized

After the sentencing each of the five magistrates
drops a gold coin into your leather purse
Before you are held down and the light leaves forever
the court offers one small last glimmer of hope

If you profess your guilt, and forgive your inquisitors
there is always the chance of the Gods' intervention

WINTER'S TALE

Near the end of a barbaric century
Of mass murder and slaughter of innocents
Winter comes to hold the landscape
Hands of death on another warm body

These monk/farmers have gone to ground
In their sanctuary to pray for lost souls
The garden, only a temporary diversion
Died its annual lingering death turning
Waxy vegetable flesh hard as glass

It reminded me of the dead in the cemetery
On their backs staring blankly at the planets
Now the earth, so hard it would be impossible
To free them from their awful weight without
Enormous fires burning on every plot

Then the thought came into my head
Do you think its easier to bury or dig up?
It's in the human condition to do one
Or the other, trying to hide or uncover

Winter holds onto the evidence until it rots
On the face of the sun in the dormant rose garden
In spring, finally, someone goes out
And ploughs the earth into careful furrows

ABBEY *Meditations*

INVOCATION

*Let it be told in a single breath
How the voice of God translated
thunder in yellow clouds*

*A hammer speaks out
on the metal roof of the sky
slanted rain drifts
towards the dusty trees*

*This is the future trapped in time
A broken spring in a machine
that will never run again rusting
in a hedge row on the open prairie*

*Sound rolls away into the distance
smell of earth left behind
Shine of leafy greenness*

PROLOGUE

From the beginning,
a ceiling of stars glitter
in the wilderness of the heavens
Imagination, only a reflection
like the white bird lying between us
or the dream of the tiger burning
under the scrawling light

On this earthy place the flowers
must be as beautiful as in paradise
Time winds down on the stem
Flowers running out of colour
and comformity bleed into the season

Now the fragile beauty of regret,
fires of frost burn in the garden
leaves fall, spinning on earth, vines
twist away underfoot in detritus
Green things turn brown and dry
Tumbleweed rolls in the wind

Icy mist falls gently in the air
unspeakable cold embraces
the sun's faint ember
Stained sky stares back
inside a bleached skull
The dream of sleep in tired eyes

FAITH

In this tribe poverty
is everything

Nothing falls
in the shadows

How sweet life
must be
wise man

UNDER THE APRICOT MOON

The dinner companions sparkled
with literary conversation about the poets
who moved out west and became movie stars
It's easy enough in pompous rhetoric
to leave the humble flatland for the good life
Not worth explaining I needed a little grit
in my life, so I traveled the other way.
Nothing to contribute, I wander out the back door
summer sliding a thick green carpet underfoot
Mosquitoes in the air humming drowsily

Four times around the running track,
slapping at the slow fliers trying for my blood
Somewhere in Muenster a dog barks at a car
a lawn mower idles in a grassy ditch
children play baseball on a gravel street
Lined with wind-dancing tree skirts
Silver spruce, pine, balsam fir, ornamental cedars
Summer on the prairies. Big window of sky
Orange dusty moonlight over yellow field
Tiny bats dart through the atmosphere

BUTTERFLY WING

Walking in the garden
it glanced off my arm

soft memory of light
a torn eye flying
an erratic pattern
in wind tousled trees,
yet, when I stopped caring

it touched down lightly
on the zucchini vine

THE ROOTS OF PIETY

When I look at his painful body,
a heavy weight pulled down
the dark corridor of time,
I think of the agony in his steps
the days he must have prayed
to be taken by his host

When he speaks to me
his eyes shine with the light of God
and I am struck to dumbness
by the peaceful attitude of his mind
pondering the history of the world
glorious summer sun blessing
the honeybees in the hive
before his billowing smoker

Make what you will of abbey trees,
in their thousands,
marching down the landscape
in straight soldier rows
His spirit flutters like a kite
played out on a fishing line
by a boy on a rough prairie field

MEDITATION ON AN EMPTY PAIL

Tonight, salmon pink clouds
float above the horizon
and I see a chariot in the sky

The white flowers in the hedge
waste themselves, day old
bloom turns to dross

The bitterness in evergreens
blackened along the edge
like a battlefield tinged by death

From a snag the lively bird
sings God's evening song
wind ruffles its feathers

BITTER WIND ON FALL TREES

A rush of yellow in the trees
paper corn dry and rustling
the wind in the tall spruce
answers my prayers

I crave snow banks,
the green wall of Northern Lights
climbing the night sky
little by little winter approaches

I waited in the dark for you
mastering the small hours
hoped you'd come again
to see the ruined garden

By Halloween, nights stiffened
a porcupine wandering in
from the forest chewed through
the salty handle on the axe

FOR HE WHO FINDS FAULT

I walk back along the ridge
to the crooked small trees

standing beside the railway track
where it bends slightly

the sun running into the shadows
touches patches of snow

by the time I return, crossing
the fallow field

bells tolling boldly in the wind
answer the silence

NIGHT OF BRAWNY STARS

I have too many memories
of the missing running away
from the past and the dead
to even consider talking
with you about the future

Your untimely arrival
upsets order in the universe
The vanishing blues
turn up again staring
out from my soup bowl

Summer is the violent
season of hunting cats
and crazy coloured flowers
Elusive bird sings
in the leafy undergrowth

Tonight to avoid your tears
I sleep in the cornfield
with earth for a pillow
wan moon among
the blanket stars

OCTOBER SONG

The bottom of the sky
dropped into morning
Grey ash from fires
ripping through
stubble fields
smudged the surface
of the shallow dugout

Every tree in the shelter belt
a permanent resident
I represent the temporal,
simply a visitor caught
up in a lifetime
reading and writing
The vine on the cemetery
hedge loosely draped
around yellow cedars
like a hangman's rope
has lost its heart
shaped leaves

Behind every wall
beneath the bricks
underneath, inside, within
All the words I can think of
about the internal of place
where days fall in order
into weeks and months
turning into decades
of prayer and contemplation
The graveyard tells the story

The monk who escaped
Vietnam by hiding
under a pile of fish
out in the courtyard
raking leaves

SHELTER BELT

Black sky
white cotton
flies in the wind
The day of rain
dusty lanes
turn into mud
Harping wind beats
the shelter belt
into a green wave
Leggy flowers fall back
against the tide

Light left the sky
for several minutes
When hail ripped
into the cornfield
a flash of lightning
lit up the bathroom
without a window
Right through
brick walls and out
the other side

When God shouts
that loud
do you listen?
I wondered
if I should light
a candle or braid
of sweetgrass
to honour
the bison
spirits

SCARECROW

Three cabbages left in the field
and the broken pumpkins that fell
off the back of the truck
An old wooden chair
waits for someone
brave enough to sit out
under the lead-lined sky

In the morning I scrape
the inside of the window
with a plastic credit card
See you wrapped in a scarf,
book in hand, wandering
the path, toward the garden

I know it's you sitting
on the chair reading among
the rotting piles of debris
Shade trees, bereft of leaves,
quiet as frozen water
Wind's knife edge
slashing at your face

DIALOGUE

Never spoke a word to me
for the best part of a year
Only nodded at my greetings
Soon I nodded in return
Why not minimize the effort
of the random chance

When I encountered him
on the trail he branched off
pushing through bush
I only saw the back of him
or he briskly passed my way
locked in mortal thought

Morning of the phone call
when the weight of the
troubled world crushed him
Divining the power of solitude
I looked far away from
the eyes of his grief

FIRST WINTER STORM

All afternoon drinking green tea
in Severin Hall. A few scattered
snowflakes fall against the window
By 4 pm, earth interred in white,
pristine light shines through
the eyehole of the universe
I am out making blotches, erasures,
skid marks on the immaculate
I walk across the snow covered landscape,
look back at my chaotic prints
The only pattern to mar perfection

What can I do? These masters
of prayer and meditation make
solemn music in ecclesiastic air
I struggle to write another decent line
The wind whistles through the trees
I breath in the bitter force of it,
relieve the agony of my weakness
I cannot empower the voices in my head
to speak to me about God, only poetry
I kneel in silence upon the white field

ANCHORITE

Many white stars
on black
winter cloth

Icy wind
flint to fire
strikes the face

Footsteps fall
silently on the
frozen path

DELIVERANCE

My prayer a fervent wish
I could change and become your favourite
role model in his bedroom slippers
letting out the cat at the same hour
every evening, enjoying safe,
unsalted, unbuttered, bowls of popcorn,
a glass of herbal tea,
before flannel sheets
and a midnight embrace

What can change
when the weather stays the same?
I'm trapped in Muenster,
wrapped in the sound
of buzzing institutional lights
another big snowstorm from the south
drifting over the highway
a white shifting landscape
fills in the margins

God's window has two eyes
one looking in
the other looking out

WITNESS

In the leaden winter, forty below
dark-limbed spruce trees with hoary beards
appear ghostly in ice fog
Even the sleepers in the graveyard,
sheltered by frosted hedges,
hear the bell banging on God's door

Down the hall Brother Gerald's canary
begins its morning song of redemption
to its alienated mate, brooding for a lover
Sudden bursts of colour sadder than the wilderness
travel down the polished linoleum

The oleander, in newly opened bloom,
reflected in courtyard windows,
trembles flamingo pink and fragrant
against the drifting veil of snow
It wouldn't last two minutes on the outside

It's a good thing the monks, devotion
and obedience sketched in their faces
like an occupational hazard,
are singing prayers for the living
The moment of truth is upon us,
"all the bare fields silent as eternity"

ONION SKINS

January wind whines and howls,
kissing off brick walls
with the vengeance
of a betrayed lover
Sound of it running away
across desolate fields

A sway-back horse
muzzled in frost
blood coursing through its lungs
stands at the rail fence
stamping in the snow

Plumes of breath float upward
or feathers
of a mythological creature
risen from the gut?

On their way to Vespers
old monks in black robes pass by
thirst of God on humble lips
discarded onion-skin faces
in the cellar of wasted winter

WINTER EPILOGUE

The end, the withering season foretold
Now it's come to this, hoarfrost covering the trees
Sun obscured by a snow sky before it can rise
Something scraping like a finger against the tin roof
The monks in the glass cathedral praying to God
Their faces are the faces of mankind; peaceful,
enraptured, benign, repulsive

Outside a raven flaps along the treeline
This is the bird of darkness and light
croaking in the wilderness above lonely fields
investigating every small possibility
God put him here on the grounds of the pious
A reminder that death's beak feasts in open
country beyond the brick walls of sanctuary

DEAR BROTHER OF GOD

You have worked yourself to the bone
giving so much for the benefit of others
You have lived to a great age
Time's constant arbitration of faith
has left you withered
and partially broken

No time to look back
there's nothing left
but a lifetime's ashes
The children, long in the grave,
faint images of laughter
for the benefit of your soul
Here man's perfection
never in doubt
God knows you as a sinner
prepares you for the far journey
to the white desert

Now he will cleanse your spirit
in the still waters of solitude
and you will be free

BUT THEN WHO AM I TO SAY

It will be as it is in this life.
When God breathes gently on tree-lined grassy pastures
the chewing, plodding, dull-thinking beasts
in their four-footed madness go out bawling
at the lovely greening of the spring
When God's voice echoes in the vaulted ceiling
the power and vision of the light of the world
reflects in morning sun on sacred windows
Trance-inducing words and sounds resonate
like the wisdom of the thinker in the desert
who sacrifices the flesh to find the spirit
The long purposeful silence of the holy man
wearing useless rags in a useless abode
poorest of the poor, utterly forgotten
absolutely powerless, "sacred in the
infinite solitude of God Himself"

Unflawed beauty of youth wasted in wars
the dead woman's pale face framed in clouds
an old man's yellow hands reaching out for God
Poverty and dissolution alive in the streets
torn and pasted together again by fear and hope
even the ones not ready to go, marked by time
by the puffing teakettle, by water running
down the drain, by the rumpled sweated sheet
in the unmade bed that lies there like a paragraph
in a novel about the dream of the permanent sleeper
who lives in the valley of the unknown
Black figures move through the dawn
voices singing for forgiveness and redemption
unworthy sinners under starred heavens
God saves us over and over again

Nobody will be perfect without omissions and errors
although some will be more so than others
When civilization demands higher ideals
the old songs and poems will be remembered
and the lives of Saints and the holy martyrs blood
painted on the walls of the centuries
the tribulations of travellers who left old lands
and went far into the wilderness of the new
The memory of those who fell into early graves
and others who disappeared into thin air
and were never found in their hiding places,
Betrayed by the evil hand in the circle of humanity
sold out for a handful of silver or for darker desires
May mercy and justice reign in the name of God
in the present and in the future hereafter

PRAISE THE QUIET SKY

O praise solitude
      and the power of prayer
sacramental sweet grass
      smudging the heart

O praise God
      for the light of the sun
the scattered seed
      the growing earth

HYMN FOR THE LAST ONE LEFT ON EARTH

This is the song of emptiness when every living thing
perishes in the burnt forest, on molten rivers of stone

the bleak song of bad water and poison air
that snuffed us, unable to breath in our beds

the victory song of nuclear power plants
black rain falling on dominate city states at war

the nautical ballad of poisoned barren seas
of cloned man-made-fish swimming in pens

the death song, anthem of the prairie farmer
under the genetic-master investors on Wall Street

the whistling tune of the traveller leaving on the bus
before the boss finds the cash missing

the song without glory that asks forgiveness
for taking more than the earth had to give

the simple song of the believer who desires paradise
but feels unworthy because of all the bloodshed

This is the bitter/sweet song at the end of time when God
sets all the birds in the sky down on a branch in heaven

EPILOGUE

*When I am gone there'll be no time
to waste among the rustling plants
no illustrated walks after midnight
when blackness grabs the stars
or spring rain falls gently on dark soil*

*These are the facts, this is the case
time always runs out or moves on
unpacking or packing its suitcase
double checking the bus schedule
waiting for the alarm clock to go off*

*Memories fade quickly enough
until they are glimpses of the known
at another time in history, when everything was different, even the weather
and the people all went away or died*

*I will not forget the shadow of the
black robe against the morning light,
passing by on the way to prayer
the wind pressed its palm against the
window glass, the door blew shut*

*Better to leave without looking back
no regrets, keep it short. Goodbye
The sun coming up again on the
rutted highway and I have gone on
to the next accidental location*